Hang Me Up My Begging Bowl

Howe Library
Shenandoah College
and
Conservatory of Music

Presented by

Mr. Bruce Souders

Books of poetry by Chad Walsh

Hang Me Up My Begging Bowl (1981)
The End of Nature (1969)
The Unknowing Dance (1964)
The Psalm of Christ (1963)
Eden Two-Way (1954)
The Factual Dark (1949)

HANG ME UP
MY BEGGING BOWL

Chad Walsh

An Associated Writing Programs Award Book

SWALLOW PRESS
OHIO UNIVERSITY PRESS
CHICAGO   ATHENS, OHIO   LONDON

Swallow Press Books
are published by
Ohio University Press
Athens, Ohio

Library of Congress Cataloging in Publication Data

Walsh, Chad, 1914–
    Hang me up my begging bowl.

    "An associated writing programs award book."
    I. Title.
PS3545.A583H3   811'.54   80-26136
ISBN 0-8040-0351-3
ISBN 0-8040-0358-0 (pbk.)

FOR EVA MY WIFE

Why do I take such long delight in you,
The mind as avid as the body? I think
Because we stand each on his honest brink;
Below, real alligators swim in plain view.

You are the primaries—yellow, blue, and red;
Conviction's vehement hyperbole.
The pastel palette comes easiest to me,
And the ambivalence of the softly said.

In you, truth is so truly true and pure
That it could hatch the complementary lie;
In me, nuance buds from nuance, till I
Could come to nothing absolute and sure.

If there were not a chasm, then no leap,
And no refreshment of our partial souls.
If it were wider, see the torrent that rolls
With gaping teeth, and plunging banks too steep

For any climb. Plato was right. By night
We cross, recross the barely crossable
Above the monsters of an abstract hell
With the certain leaps of love. And there is light.
And being one, we see with single sight.

CONTENTS

VIII

1

COURTESY

"I must request Your Highness to place her head
Upon this block, and kindly to forgive
The gross familiarity of this axe."
"It has been well honed, I trust?"
"You couldn't ask a sharper blade.

"Fit for a queen." "You are experienced at this trade?"
"Apprenticed as a boy. Why, ma'am, a fleck of rust—
My master whipped me black and blue."
"See that you train your prentices as well."
"That I will do. I have a promising lad—

"Good, steady grip, aim as true as the Creed."
"Then all is well.
A fine young fellow for the lesser barons."
"Your Highness hears the first stroke of a bell?"
"You may proceed."

WIDENED TO THE CONGO

After the slaveship's hold
They blinked and shivered in the Georgia breeze.
Around them swirled a new world, paler than Arab traders.
Quickly the auction priced
Husband and wife and child, severed and sold.

The overseer's whip embossed the English alphabet
In red on black. And Christ
Wept by a Jordan widened to the Congo.
Bluer than indigo, softer than cotton, rose
The singing voices. Sweat

Buttered their corn pone, and the banjo's clang
Watered the northern eyes of Foster's Old Black Joes.
Were you there? I was there.
I crucified the Lord on rakes and hoes.
Between the hammer blows that drove the nails, He sang.

POTS AND KETTLES

The Land of Canaan was the promised land.
The Cains that came were good at felling forests,
Driving the Redskins to the setting sun
With subsidies of fences; triangular trade—
Niggers, molasses, rum. Some read their Walter Scotts
And some their Bibles. Few could understand

The latter Abels—famished Irish and their priests,
Germans with turnvereins and socialist plots,
Italians Mafia-trained for prohibition,
The crafty Chinese laying western rails,
The Japanese with picture brides and Shintō feasts,

The avid Jews in triple field of force: the shtetl,
Brooklyn, and Tel Aviv. The melting pots
Of school and media cooked a common sauce.
The bones and gristle were resistant lumps.
And on another burner, the blackly seething kettle.

WHEN OLD JOE LAID HIS BANJO DOWN

When old Joe laid his banjo down
The mansion peeled its paint and swayed,
The red earth weeded into ruin.

There was a drabbing of the sun,
And guestly beds were left unmade
When old Joe laid his banjo down.

From hills of scrub the cedars ran,
Sank roots of wrath and sootly stayed.
The red earth weeded into ruin.

And garden brights were overrun
By slinks of snake in hiss of shade
When old Joe laid his banjo down.

And father fell and buried son,
And gambling debts remained unpaid.
The red earth weeded into ruin.

And Snopes came snoopsing with his gun,
And mansion grayed in raid of fade
When old Joe laid his banjo down
And red earth seeded into ruin.

THEY ARE COMING BETWEEN US, ROBERT HAYDEN

They are coming between us, Robert Hayden.
They hate us both.

Ann Arbor,
Long ago,
Long evenings,
When we put aside the assigned readings,
The outlines for seminar papers,
And talked poetry,
Your poetry and mine.

Your face was rich tan,
Mine shading to olive.
The years before us
Opened out like a fan
With the news of the first poem published somewhere,
The hope of a book.

Woven into all poems
Your wife and mine,
Erma and Eva.

They are coming between us, Bob Hayden.
White power,
Black power,
Backlash,
Blacklash.

The mad taxonomies—
Skin, hair, lips.

They are saying
Classify yourself.
You are already classified.
Stand where you belong.

They are coming between us, Bob.

We are too old to learn to hate.
Let us be too young to learn to fear.

If they herd us into our separate tribes
In the guerrilla jungles of the city streets,
May Baha'u'llah and Jesus strengthen us
To drop our blasphemous guns
For the private council
Where each says to each
When's your next book coming out?
And I ask about Erma
And you about Eva.

ON HAVING A DOOR HELD OPEN FOR ME

She held the door open for me
And therein lies much history.
She held the door and I walked through
With "Thanks" and smile for howdydo,
And she smiled back a civil greeting.
It lasted me for the whole class meeting.

The reason I was taken aback
Is she was female, young, and Black.
I'd held the door often for her
And she had frowned like a racial slur.
And when I held it, so what then?
It is a habit with southern men,
And I am southern or I was,
And add to that an extra clause—
The northern liberal veneer
That made me dash from far and near
To prove to me I wasn't racial.
But she was racial, also glacial,
Until despite my pasty skin
She held the door and let me in.

Perhaps my sideburns turned the day—
Shaggy and salt and pepper gray.
Perhaps at some time she was told
To help the crippled and the old.
No matter, for the fact is true—
She held the door, Whitey walked through.

Civilization is always fragile
And keeps alive by keeping agile.
Its tonics are white lies and gray,
Sonnets and classical ballet,
Polysyllabic words, perfume,
Deodorants, a private room,
The rituals of church and state,
Sexual foreplay, patience to wait,
And most of all a door held wide
To let some civil soul inside.

THE GRANT WOOD GOTHIC TURKS

Where are the young, young Turks
I knew when I spoke their tongue?
Admirers of Edmund Burke's
And Buckley's. And some of the young

Young Turks are manning the slits
Of the fortress walls of committees
And scoring their melted-lead hits
On the raiders from radical cities.

They no longer look like Turks.
Their Grant Wood Gothic faces
Are as stern as Scottish kirks
Or Nixon's pious grimaces.

Shall I try my Turkish out
On the newest assistant professors?
They reply in a Chinese shout,
Or murmur in Spanish, "Che bless us."

KENT

1

The tears of God slant from the heavenless sky.
I sit in my studio at Yaddo,
Sodden with consciousness and conscience.
Though a grown man, I have wept sometimes,
Dallas and Memphis, but this day
Too many slaughters, too many lies
Have drained the rain clouds of my eyes.

Gray sky presses down,
Fog moves up the branches of the drenched pines.

2

I read their names in the morning *Times*—
Schroeder and Scheuer, Miller and Krause—
Bland as my class rolls—
And their first names—William, Sandra, Jeffrey,
And Allison, my daughter's name.

Fog enfolds my studio.
Nothing to see, nowhere to go.

Brain and heart an empty hull,
My Lai rotting in my skull.

Four names writhing in a row,
Four students I shall never know.

3
They were not, it appears, hippies, effete snobs,
Or bums. If President or Vice-President had met them,
Almost they might have approved, though Jeff's hair
Needed some orderly attention. There was nothing by Mao
    or Che
In his room, but a soft-cover *Lost Horizon* for a President's
    bedside reading.

Sandy, "happy kid, always the one who made jokes,"
You stood up too soon from the shelter of parked cars,
Too young to believe how long horror can last.
Bullet in the neck on the way to speech therapy class,
You who might have liberated our tongues
Stuttering with a decade's obscenity.

Bill, with the haircut of an Eagle Scout,
Captain of cross-country team at Lorain High School,
Trumpet player, second in ROTC,
You idly watched the advance of your brother Guardsmen.
How desperate a fratricide to gun you down.

Allison, with the face of a young Madonna,
Whose dark eyes search me from a newsprint halftone,
Good Jewish daughter, loving a Jewish boy,
You dropped beside him, your class canceled forever.

4

Fog seeps in through window frames.
I damply repeat the four dead names.

This was no Easterday uprising
To set a new Yeats sermonizing.

Say simply that they chanced to die
For reasons distant as My Lai.

Set their names down one by one:
Bill...Sandy...Jeff...and Allison.

2

SAPPHICS

See the rain slants, randomly aimed like napalm,
Just and unjust equally bare to free fire.
Dulled by drought's blockade, all the blades of grass blaze
    Flickering greenly.

Heat of rain melts final debris of snowhumps.
Hearing heat beat drumming the earthern rooftop
Mole and chipmunk clamber from winter houses
    Brownly consenting.

I PUT THE SPLIT BEECH

I put the split beech in the cradle of kindling,
Light the newspaper. The fire has its way,
Paper to kindling to quarters of beech.

As evening falters to bed
The last coals burn gray and powdery.
Only once or twice before sleep takes me
I see the flickering shadows on the wall.
There has been strong entropy this night.

In the morning, the ashes.
I shovel them out, scatter them into the woods,
Saying perhaps a secular prayer:
May they feed the roots of new beeches.

I suppose I should pray first of all
To the sun, but the sun is too far
For a neighborly prayer. I'll settle for beeches
And tend their roots with the ashes of beeches.

MEDITATION ON AMANITA VERNA

Here nature apes technology. This mushroom,
Risen, it seems overnight, by the curving
Of the wooded path to my study,
Stands in solitary chastity
Brushing against my shoe as I go past.

It is pure form. Compass and straightedge sketched it.
A dread hand filled it with concentrated death.
This white angel is the destroyer. Death
Is as close at hand and handy
As plucking fingers and a curious bite.

It is as beautiful and chaste as death,
Chaste as the cylinder and hemisphere
That sprouted from the heart of Hiroshima.
It is the poor man's private atom bomb,
Free for himself and packaged for his neighbors.

I go into my study. New poems, half naked,
Sprawl on my desk, their pubic hair too public,
Awaiting the fig leaves of crafty revision.
I set to work. If these sweating sluts refuse me,
The virgin offers a delayed and final orgasm.

THE WARNINGS ARE SO MILD I COULD ALMOST
UNSAY THEM

The warnings are so mild I could almost unsay them,
Now in the stasis of days forever and brief.
A leaf or branch here and there
Blood red or fire red,
Melancholy lavender of wild asters by little brooks.
But the sky is blue,
The lake is June mild for swimming.

Here on my desk
The ponderous heap of notes
For the heavy book I didn't write this summer
And a slighter heap to take home
Of poems to revise.

I put the tarpaper screens in the bright window frames.
The clear sun beats
And drowsy warmth fulfills the little house.

I think if I stayed,
The calendar and clock would never fidget.

Drowsiness would take me.

Late autumn would infiltrate unnoticed.

I would sleep with the winter fish
Beneath the feet of ice on the frozen lake.

20

SEAL ON THE BEACH

A less than human but more than animal roar,
And the great jaws opening in outrage
To an almost perfect circle. The seal,
Stranded by low tide on the tourist beach,
Stares straight into my camera with furious eyes
And almost stares it down.

The camera clicks. "Shotgun," the ranger says.
"Fishermen got him." I see the blood flecks,
Specks of rust patterned down the great body.
"A law against it?" "Yes, but they compete.
Seals and fishermen after the same fish."
The flippers stir clumsily.

The great body moves in a waddle of walk
Like astronauts testing an airless moon.
At water's edge he gives a speeding lunge.
The surf receives him into the grace of water.
Swimming fast to deep sea,
He diminishes in our binoculars.

Fishermen have mortgage payments every month,
They send their children to the yearly dentist,
Empty a can of beer and watch TV.
The shotgun is the final rationing system.
I dream of an ocean of infinite fish
And the fraternal clasp of hand and flipper.

The seal has faded to a bobbing dot.
"He won't last long," the ranger says.
"He's prey to anything that comes along."

LAMENT FOR A FALLEN WAXWING

A compound fracture in its trailing wing,
The cedar waxwing slept his final night,
A matchstick for a splint, a piece of string

To hold it tight. Chokeberries red and bright,
Mulberries royal on an old tin plate
Vainly encouraged him to take a bite.

He was too new and young to have a mate.
His first flight was, perhaps, his only one.
His body stiffened to the feathers' weight.

The children buried him where flecks of sun
Dappled through clumps of birches. On the dock
The hordes of ordered ants muster and run

To programed destinations. On the rock
Ten feet from shore a seagull stalks and preens.
High overhead I see a circling hawk.

A chorused mating song flutes from the trees,
And Megan sits alone with stricken eyes
And knowledge seventy years will not appease:

That in this world a waxwing falls and dies.

ECOLOGICAL AFTERMATH

The Armageddon of the Biosphere—
That's what the minstrels call it in their ballads—
Was not one certain day, professors tell us—
At least the songs I hear the minstrels sing
Jumble the times and skip from year to year

And back again, to fit their jangling rhymes.
They say the ocean died of poisoning.
The gasping dwellers of the hills and mountains
Not instantly but yearly more and more
Tumbled into the plains, and bloody times

There were, as armies fought for air and land
With the last hoard of liquid coal, and ore,
Bang of exploding stars, toadstools of fire,
Devils' castles blazing. And then the pest
No doctor's vial or spell could countermand.

The minstrels say blotched bodies clogged the streams
Till in the stinking sea they came to rest,
Drifting like rotten rafts where the currents took them.
Horned heads and claws for hands and forked tails twitching
Capered in dawn dances from poisoned dreams.

My father's father's father made this clearing
With an iron axe revealed by powerful witching
In a dream of stones piled in a shapeless mound.
He carved a wooden plowshare, kissed and stirred
The rooted earth, gave his seeds a good smearing

Of toad blood in the darkness of the moon,
And when the crop was eaten by a herd
Of unicorns, he drove a fence of stakes,
Sharp and a man's height high, around his earth
And reaped a holy crop of corn. And soon,

My father's father says, no one saw unicorns
Again, though that straight horn above the hearth—
My father found it caught in a hollow tree—
But now the night soil acolytes are coming,
Singing their hymns and blowing on their horns—

Blessèd be the soil of night for the crops of day,
Blessèd be the upper and the lower intestines,
Blessèd be the chamber pot, the chalice of our prosperity,
Blessèd be Mother Earth and helpful worm,
Blessèd be Father Sun who draws the corn stalk upward,
Blessèd be the cobs of corn, gift of the kindly Gods;
Cursèd be he who changes the numbers of the periodic table,
Cursèd be he who poisons Mother Earth with alchemy,
Cursèd be he who stirs the Mother with a blade of iron,
May his name be blotted from the transcript of the Gods
    forever;
Blessèd be the soil of night for the crops of day,
Bless Mother Earth and Father Sun world without end. Amen.

I really ought to be an acolyte.
That's the first step to a professorship.
Then I could learn to read the altar entrails,
Put spells on the Gods' enemies and mine,
And kill or kiss the devils of the night.

I never was good at memorizing charts.
The periodic table—I stopped with the first line.
Well, the professors say God needs us, too,
To plant the corn and tend the cows and swine,
And they will specialize in the liberal arts.

3

THE ANGLE OF MY EYES

The angle of my eyes
Slanting upward
To the rim of your skirt.

And far above,
Creation's first fire
When you opened the kitchen range.

And from the window
The cornfield climbing the mountain
And the scarecrow in the middle of the cornfield.

World of terror
And terrified delight.

In archaic smallness
I watched the scarecrow forever.

LIE ON THE WOODEN PLANKS OF THE FLOOR

Lie on the wooden planks of the floor
At the end of the porch
Near the strings of morning glories
Closed and crumpled
For the night.

Just as I am, without one plea.

The water runs
One way forever in the river.
The kerosene lamp
In the living room
Sends a road of light through the window,
Plays on my drowsy toes.

Rock of ages, cleft for me.

The river flows beyond the garden.
The colored Baptists baptize new souls
In the river
Twice a year.
In the mudflats the dark willows sing low.

Brother, tiptoe around me.
I am close to sleep.
The honeysuckle from the fence
Floats me,
Sinks me,
Tide of sleep.

Shall we gather at the river?

There is a room of mysteries
Where Mama and Daddy scream.
There is a door that slams open,
Shut.
The car roars,
Tires skid on gravel.

Baptists sing softly now.
The bedroom is silent now.

Abide with me.

Brother,
Take me in your arms.
Hold me in the honeysuckle of the night.

THE YEAR BEFORE I STARTED FIRST GRADE

The year before I started first grade
The town council passed a sanitary ordinance.
Our landlord was outraged.
This was creeping socialism.
The old one had served generations.
The pit was only half full.
He might have to raise our rent.
It was the government
And those damned doctors.

Law was law.
He sent in a workman
Who dug a four-foot pit
In a corner of the vegetable garden.
I would stand at the edge
Smelling the clean clay,
Looking at the four sharp sides,
Thinking
If I fell in
The top of my head would just about be level with the ground.

Autumn slipped by
In a wither of frosted tomato vines,
A flush of brightening leaves,
While I watched the workman
Erecting the legal little house,
A conventional two-holer
Except for the newfangled ventpipe on top.

One day we trained ourselves to take a new path
Through the bedraggled tomato vines and hallowe'en cornstalks.

The old one still stood
But was against the law now.
It was six weeks before the old spiders
Learned to circumambulate under the new oval openings.

We carried Sears to the new house,
Finished the newsprint pictures first.
I studied them carefully so I would recognize
All the things I never hoped to buy,
Then like hopes so modest
They had no names
The sheets would drop one by one
Into the pit.

Poverty was not too keen
Until the winds of January and February
Blew through the cracks of the new little house,
Bringing the season of slick paper
And colored illustrations.

A very long time,
Watched by the doleful spider weaving a ladder beside me,
I stared at the bright images,
Knowing I would learn from them
Only the slick touch of poverty.

All the costly items in Sears
That went at last into the cold pit of wanhope.

I HATED MY FATHER

I hated my father.
On the weekends he came home
He and mother screamed at each other in the bedroom.
At dinnertime,
Only we called it supper,
They talked of money money money.

I feared my father.
On the rare weekends he came home
He talked about discipline,
Promised to whip me,
Never stayed long enough to do it.

I hated and feared my father.
He wanted to start a rooming house in West Virginia.
He wanted me to be the waiter,
Said I would get ten-cent tips from the boarders,
He was an insurance agent.
That was respectable.
Only colored people took tips.

I hated my father.
He came home some weekends.
I hated him more
When he stopped coming.

The grocer cut off our credit in a penciled note
Delivered with our last order
By the consumptive neighbor boy who dragged the little wagon.
We waited out one long weekend on a can of beans
And apples I stole in a farmer's pasture.
A $5 check came from my brother that Monday,
The one who was married and had a wife to support.

When my father still came home
I remember one Friday
I hunted him out at the pool room.
He showed me off.
I could do big sums in my head.
I loved him.
I asked him for a quarter
To buy some water colors.
He gave it to me.
He was tall by the pool table among the tall men.

I hated my father.
I would wake up in sweating underwear,
Thinking I heard him on the porch.
Sometimes I dreamed of my father
At night
On a horse,
A white one,
Riding through the front door
To spank me,
To lift me high,
To take me to the grocery store,
To drive me home
With a big bag of groceries between us.

In dreams
I would have followed him to West Virginia.

I hated, I feared, I loved
My father.
I was a father three times over
When I learned he was dead,
A month gone,
Pneumonia,
In a rooming house in Norfolk,
Lonely, dead, buried.

Some day if I dare
I shall visit his grave.

THE AIR RIFLE I WANTED

The air rifle I wanted
Arrived that Christmas.
It would send a round pellet
Fifty yards or more.

Once I hit the target's center.
Targets don't move.
There was no sport in this.

One day, a flight of finches
Gold ebony
Ebony gold
Under white puffs of cloud.

I shot at them in general.
One
Fluttered
Dropped.
The others flew indifferently on.

One finch fluttered
Like a paper airplane,
Landed in small bushes
By the rail fence.

I walked to the thicket.
The glittering unaccusing unforgiving
Eyes.
Broken wing.
Ooze of blood.

I took a stick,
Hit it harder
Than mere death required.

I hit it again and again.
Focus faded from the ebony eyes.

The deed had to be done
And quickly done
And thoroughly done
Or never done.

WHEN AUTUMN CAME

When Autumn came,
The pear tree in our chicken yard,
Memory of white stars of lace
And the officious bees,
Dropped a heaviness,
Gold and russet,
Heart shape,
Secret of love.

I would put one pear in my overall pocket,
Walk the two miles to the certain tulip poplar
By the old rail fence near the tenant farmer's house.
Russet and gold,
Inverted heart of love.
I would stand by the straight trunk
Looking through big lace of gold and russet
Up the long bole
To the tip I could almost see.

Slowly
As though it were a sacrament
I would eat the pear.

As I walked home
I would look back and wonder
How would the tree appear
If I climbed eighty feet
And looked down.

I never climbed the tree.
I walked the two miles home
And ate the gold and russet
Mosaics of the chicken yard.

PEPPE

The U.N. citizen,
Evenly poised between one year and two,
Asks *Dov'è Mamma,* rejects his milk with an *All done,*
Babbles mostly in Basque,
Speaks clearest with a hug and hug again.

In his assembly of the double helices
All have the right to ask
The world's regard: the Roman orator,
The Phrygian trader and the Nubian slave,
And peering from the trees

Of Northern Lights the German, the red-haired Celt.
Perhaps along the line of time the Mongol gave
A helix of remembrance.
His chubby arms spiral into a wave.
I twirl the universe of helices and melt.

ON BUILDING A CRADLE FOR CHAD WALSH HAMBLIN

The lumber yard had nothing fit to build it.
I searched our attic. A house as old as this one
Has everything if you will keep on looking.
I found the wide pine shelves, century old,
As though the stars or doting gods had willed it.

My sabre saw rounded the simple curves,
I drilled the holes for wooden pegs to hold
The planks as one; I glued the rockers on,
And tested it, as smooth a lulling motion
As the tide's swell to soothe a baby's nerves.

Sleep, little Chad,
Between the auburn boards upon the ocean
Of father's, mother's love and mine.
Rock to whatever hand sets love in motion.
Sleep, little Chad.

4

ZIHUATANEJO

See where the other waiter, our favorite,
Feeds a banana to that small-bit actor,
The improbable iguana on the terrace wall.
Bikinis briefly blossom in the warm pool;
Two peacocks strut like tropical flowers on feet.

Glass-green water from farther than Japan
Knowingly strokes the sloping beach to a roil
Of gray sand in white breakers a few yards out;
An undertow offers the masque of harmless rape
To me, now Tiresias, once a man.

RETROSPECT

The times—or I—were out of joint.
I was not strong enough to turn the times about.
Perhaps I should have learned to shout.
I settled for the counterpoint

Of the ironic Southern voice
And commented with rhymes upon the passing scene.
And sixty times the trees raged green
And gold again. I made my choice.

A Shakespeare (Marlowe at the least)
Surveyed the titan stage, and heard the surging roar
Of blank verse breaking on my shore.
I heard the silence when he ceased.

The sherry hour, love's hour of bed,
The sonnet sequence and the formal elegy
Floated upon an inland sea.
The trees have dried to gold and red.

ASCENSION

Suspended in a kind of time and space,
I saw them hide your face
And wrap me in a second sheet
From head to feet.
The crumpled car, delivered of its load,
Slumped in the middle of the road
Until with flashing lights and clanging chains
They freed the road of its remains.

To be a nowhere and a naught
Was not a goal that I had sought,
But as I floated there, suspended,
And everything was ended,
I thought how easily the thing was done.
And now the sun
Shone on the narrowing tape
Twisting through wooded mountains with a serpent's shape.

High now, my scanning sight
Saw Cuba on my right,
And to the left was Hudson's Bay
With little seals at play.

The far earth slowly turned.
The far sun slowly burned.

Over the Adirondacks was a local shower.
The Great Lakes glistened like five petals of a flower.

CURTAIN CALL

Five acts at most they have. Meekly they die—
Whatever act and scene the author chooses—
By rope or sword, pillow or asp. They lie
Like scattered logs upon the stage. One loses
The total tally with the stretch of time.
Trumpets or cannon or a poor, maimed rite
Ushers them off and down. Virtue and crime
Share their six feet of noncommittal night.

Down, curtain. Up. Lady Macbeth serves tea
To Duncan. Richard and little princes romp.
Ophelia scampers up a willow tree.
The Egyptian rises with accustomed pomp.
Lear and Cordelia sing a song of willow.
The Moor and bride divide their common pillow.

REFLECTIONS IN THE COURSE OF AN AVERAGE DAY

1
When I wake up
At six o'clock or ten o'clock
The long day stares me in the face
And stares me down
When I wake up.

The weight of more than half a century,
The idiot brightness of the risen sun,
The sound of trucks going important places,
My neighbor's radio, the morning news—
God, what a century!

When I wake up at six or ten o'clock
I resurrect the prison pair of shoes,
Align them as twin wardens of the day,
And put one limp foot (whose?)
Into the sad sack of a morning sock.

2
How far away they seem,
The grandfathers, grandmothers,
Crotchety sometimes or benign,
Loquacious with tales of San Juan Hill
Or rocking silent with a sixty-year dream.

We listened to them and their stories
Or if we did not listen we kept still
And when they gave us good advice
We murmured in polite assent
While dreaming of our future sins and glories

In a Camelot of the fabled North
Of Mason-Dixon, where some miraculous event
Or fact of climate would keep us young forever.
And in due course to New York or Wisconsin we went
Where I sit dreaming, talking, rocking back and forth.

3
The search for pirate gold
Has ended, and the substitution ciphers
Are put aside, or sold to children to keep them busy.
Now common sense, disease
Of time, has pocked us. We are growing old.

We often said, then let it come and no great matter,
But now the secular trees
Usurp the acres of the sacred grove.
I have my favorite chair and thank you not to take it.
The raindrops are a patter

Of secret agents from a coming age.
The raftered roof needs little wind to storm and break it.
Tonight, a score of seasons,
The green earth tilting straight when we forsake it,
Then dream or not to dream, each in his private cage.

4
Am I a stunted growth?
I always thought the old were holding back
Some secret—wisdom, power, the secret's very name—
But now I'm old or nearly
And haven't any secret word or oath.

Whatever I have learned, I gladly share, but mostly
The young already clearly
Know it, or else it doesn't matter greatly.
The very old are close-lipped as the very young.
I feel diffused and ghostly.

48

And God Himself is holding out on me,
Hushing the prayers that once came gushing from my tongue.
Silent among the silent,
Haunted by all the tunes I have not sung,
I caulk small boats of verse for every stranger's sea.

5
Dull little ego, I have squeezed you dry.
You've had your say, confiding to bored ears
Your twitches of regret and celebration,
A few quick seconds of illumination,
Usual terrors. Ego, thou shalt die.

Henceforth be nothing fact nor with an address.
Where mere I was, arise imagination,
Breeding like Abram's seashore-sanded scions,
Till the bright souls of all I have never been
Don flesh and clothes, and instant wings caress

The rising currents of the singing air.
Ascend, ye wings, beat harder where the thin
Molecules falter. Escape from gravity
To colonize the raging sands of Mars.
I am not there nor here nor anywhere.

5

ON READING THOMPSON'S BIOGRPAHY OF
ROBERT FROST
                    for Howard Munford

You were vain and vicious as we all are
Who craftily devise the words to dance
On empty graves. I spent two hours with you.
You waved Tom Eliot to his desert, praised
Harmless mediocrities, still raced
West-running brook against remote Spoon River.

From your friends who knew to bat hard but wild
When you pitched, from your chosen Boswell and
      his notebooks
And resentments, we say we know you now,
And we stand a little straighter, seeing you twisted.

The loaded pistol hidden but handy, the rooms
Of silence, insanity, and suicide,
The private letters written to your critics,
The conspiratorial notes to Untermeyer.

I hope death took you in mercy's sudden ambush,
For none more fought and feared the common foe.
Perhaps you breathed your last in a bright dream
Of the Derry farmhouse, or by a black brook
Flung backward on itself in one white wave.

If there's a limbo of natural happiness
Where every poet receives a monthly Nobel
And each believes his is the only prize,
Where each declaims his verses to the circle
And does not hear the other circling voices,
And you are young again and Elinor speaks—

53

I leave you there. You went miles, kept promises,
Raging always to the soul's last West Northwest.
I do not read you. I will read your book,
Drink and be whole again beyond confusion.

IN MEMORY OF W.H. AUDEN—SEPTEMBER 29, 1973

My Damaris (then two,
Now old as he was then)
Do you remember?

Your toys covered the floor
When he rang the bell at six,
Forgetful if dinner was six or seven.
"Better early than late," he apologized,
And knelt on the floor beside you,
Helping put chaos back into its box.

Your brown eyes dilated double
At his Oxford accent.

Remember and praise.

He left us in late September,
The full and fall of the year.
They found him gone
In a Viennese hotel.

He was no smashed Berryman,
No gassed Plath.
More wrinkled than Father Time,
He expected an Act of God,
The Father's absurd timetable.
The hour was a little early.

He was sincere and civilized.
He wore sincerity lightly
So that to some it was invisible
And only the bristling skin of his wit
Registered in their inferior cameras.

An integrated liberal, he was a wicked foe
To liberal bombast and linguistic tics.
At a table of certified academics
He called the candles "nigger lights"
And added that in his father's house
Tradesmen and Baptists used the back door.
He inquired of his hostess,
"Why do they always give me rice
When everyone knows I'm a potato man?"

At a forum of future teachers of America,
When asked by an anxious young woman,
"If you gave an assignment
And a pupil said, 'I won't do it,'
What would you do?"
His flat voice replied,
"I would whip that child"
And waited for further questions.

By some crossing of the genetic code
Or hormone imbalance
Or God knows what Freudian plot—
Or plain, personal preference—
His flesh kept its distance from women.
When he came to town for a reading
He abandoned the legendary prizes
To Dylan Thomas and the epigoni
Of the bar and bedroom.
Sedate and faithful,
Like an old married man,
He lived with Chester Kallman,
And never revised the Bible to prove it right.

56

Like all civilized men,
He honored the value of money,
Knowing it could buy, for instance,
An extra room to his Austrian farmhouse.
And money was his intention
Ten years ago when at $600
An evening ($200 for the agent)
He made the six-weeks marathon
Of the Midwest circuit.

He asked to stay with us.
We were familiar Ann Arbor faces,
Eva an adequate mother figure.
And it saved money.
Each day he ate less,
And drank more,
Surviving on red wine and future orientation.

Returning from an ex-teachers'-college,
"Pumpkins!" he shouted,
"They are nothing but pumpkins!"

I drove him to the bus station next morning
And Austria was in his eyes.

Never a father and accordingly
Never a grandfather,
He was every civil man's godfather,
A benign and prickly presence,
Proclaiming in tolerant rhythms
That though everything in particular
Is after the Fall,
Everything in general is right.

His early admirers never forgave him
When he annexed Marx and Freud
To Kierkegaard and Jesus.
This was trahison aux clercs
Who had reeled a decade
With Eliot's apostasy.
They spoke of a passing phase.
The years passed.
I set the clock at six
To drive him to early Mass.
They never knew that only the light-tongued
Can sincerely say the Nicene Creed.

Though he begot no sons,
He was fecund of poems
And murderous as a Roman father,
Decreeing which should be exposed.
His abandoned children
Huddled in the exile of alien anthologies
Like Latvian embassies in compassionate capitals.

He never presumed his soul was interesting.
He confessed to a priest, not a paying public.
He assumed that in the eyes of an amused God
A poet is rather like a carpenter,
Bungling sometimes of course,
But useful in a minor way
As one who articulates and nails together
The boards of the fragile and ever falling City,
Staying for a time the lapse to mere nature.

Now that he is dead
Real rats scurry overhead.
Now that he is gone
Termites sample wood and stone.

He was the last of the modern masters;
He is gone where Yeats, Frost, Pound, Eliot, and Roethke are,
The least paranoid of the lot, or the one who best hid it.
Now we are left, one supposes, with Lowell
In a long decline of limp sonnets.

Little Austria, stripped of Empire,
Suited him well. Peaceful by necessity,
It practiced the small arts of civility
And earned money by being old and beautiful.

He looked so old he was dateless
Like a bust in millennia of rain
And eroded by furrows of hail.

All that the passing clock
Could do to a face it had done.
The whetted mind of the tongue
Sang Agapè's surgical song.

6

EPITHALAMIUM FOR CHARLIE AND ALISON

Shout loud, you seagulls of the soaring sky;
You modest thrushes of the forest, sing.
Come, booming frogs, forsake the cozy cove
And in this temple form a heart-shaped ring.
Silent chipmunks, raise up your tails on high.
All creatures, greet the dawn and day of love.

You sun, on green leaves of our energy,
Shine brighter in the glory of this day.
And crickets, chirp the earth's renewing tune.
And butterflies, ascend to heavenly play.
Peer from your mask inside the hollow tree,
Raccoon. The god and goddess stand here soon.

Here's fine reversal. See Eros dark and deep
As moonbeams through the twigs of rustling night,
And Aphrodite bright as blazing sun.
Know love is such, for darkened out of sight
It has a secret only two can keep,
The stars that searched the earth when earth began.

Sweet stars, still burning from creation's day,
Sing counterpoint that two alone can hear,
The harmony that tunes the wastes of space.
Seagulls and thrushes, louder. The gods appear.
Frogs, boom. And chipmunks, frolic at your play.
Raccoon, a dance. Love stands here face to face.

IN THE MEADOW OF THE GARDEN OF THE SQUIRREL

In the meadow of the garden of the squirrel,
The oxeye daisies, the Indian paint brush,
The buttercup, the clover, the other tinted lives
Sway in the stroking breeze.
Sometimes they touch,
Like to like,
Borrowing small rapid wings or the wings of wind.
There will be flowers for another year.

They are invincible and frail,
Frail to the feeding cattle,
Frail to my clumsy boots,
Frail to the hurricane
Growling a thousand miles south in its Caribbean cage,
Frail at last to the tilt of a globe
That will standardize their bright signals to dull
Into a darkness that white snow will annul.

They are frail and invincible.
There will be flowers for another year.
They will brighten among the tumbled stones
Of Washington's marble monuments.

Walk with me among the spring flowers.
The breeze that brushed your breast
Strokes my hand.
Let us do only good to each other
While the bright energy of the sun
Shines on our quick radiance.

VACUOUS BLISS

The Easterners know it, always have.
The many cells returning
To the unitary spot of consciousness
Where light and darkness, plenitude and emptiness
Are one, where the godhead and the primal amoeba
Gape in vacuous bliss and know nothing,
Are nothing, are all.

Forsaking mathematics,
The sonnet form, committee structures,
The passions of bifurcated sex, affirming
Only the number one, and the fiction
Of zero, I suppose I too, with training,
Could crawl beneath the flaming arms of angels
Back into that fragrant paradise
That was our first and favorite heaven.
And likely enough, time and I will choose it.
After how many thousand karmas, after
The roll call of successive births, weanings, weddings,
And the shadow play of deathbed scenes,
Time and I will grow weary together,
And with a last reach of my special hand
I will lead you, beloved, to that forever
Where you and I, God and Gandhi,
Christ and the amoeba are one and all and nothing.

It will come to this, O beloved,
But not yet. Not yet.

LUNAR LOVE

1

The moon and back,
How many times this shuttle run.
We've stayed as long
As earthly oxygen would let,
Almost to the coming of the black.

We've thought of Mars, to be first and stake our claim,
But left it so far to the Houston set
And their metallic unmanned probes.
Venus would not content us. Jupiter
Remains, and Pluto of the ominous name.

I've come back home to colonize my memories—
The day Damaris was born and I looked at her,
That earlier day when you first smiled into my eyes,
A pine grove and the wind and we astir.
Come let us walk into the nighttime of the trees.

2

No circling spaceprobe spying on the moon
Has memorized a surface half as fully
As I your skin,
Though with touch only I survey the craters,
The maria, and mountains of your skin.

And I have studied, too, subsurface forces
And other scientific matters
(The heart no probe can pierce still keeps its mystery),
Learned to provoke, by hand to plotted zones,
Legs twisting with the force of unnumbered horses;

Twin knolls reshaping at light spanks;
The lesser twins, volcanoes with live cones;
The mid abyss where subject and object are one;
Tides of the hot core, unscientific moans.
Thus I publish my researches and give thanks.

3
We colonized the earth. We aimed for the moon.
Like Everest, it was there.
And there it hung before us, gray and white,
Sculpted with cruel craters and peaks.
For no good reason we would be landing soon.

A slight seizure, power failing, dials dropping,
A fog of oxygen from unprogramed leaks.
We circled round the moon of theory
And aimed our arc for the blue-white disk of earth
Of the temperate continents and rain clouds dripping.

Into the incredible sea we parachuted down.
Only in sleep do I circle forever in a ring
To breathe each last time the gasping oxygen,
Or on a long ellipse to blaze and fling
My body into the thermonuclear sun.

4
The silver flecks of moon
Like shining dust patterned by rocket thrust
Rise and glide on the rippling lake in grids of light
Until it seems our bed
Floats the coordinates of astral noon.

Armstrong, Aldrin, Collins, this trinity
Flew far to fringe your head
With the pure radiance of another sphere,
And thirty lengths from earth I travel with one kiss
Upon the tranquil sea

Of the dark hollow of your cheek. Sleep sound,
Diana, huntress of my sleep, chaste Artemis;
My blinded eyes have found
The light that lighted me into the world.
Beyond the world and in the world. I am homeward bound.

TERRESTRIAL LOVE

1

For everything under the sun, a time, a reason.
Coffee and toast at breakfast,
Christ's body for my dinner once a week,
Cocktails or wine at 5:00 o'clock,
And the dark sweetness of your body when in season.

Time for the secular city and a time for prayer,
A time to open doors, a time to lock,
A time for picket lines, a time for writing verse,
A time to lay you down in darkness
To be the ground bass to the singing air.

I never say a prayer before I love you.
I offer simple human strength and weakness.
I think that God commends our privacy.
Or if God's dead, my back will bear the bleakness
Of cold nothing. You have me above you.

2

Snow falling steadily, the keen wind seeping
Under the door and round the window frames.
A glacial age infiltrates our square fortress,
Assuming all things to the entropy
Of random energy and time frozen and sleeping.

Our weapons of defense are three and frail:
A furnace burning the sun's young energy
From jungles of the age of dinosaurs;
The furnace of the stomach burning bright
A little sun of meat; and if these fail,

Come close to me. The battery of love,
Charged with the energy of another light—
Perhaps that far gleam from creation's rim
Where galaxies still sing the first day's hymn—
Is good, I swear it, for a last warm hour of love.

3
You are as fragile as an hypothesis
In physics. Like the ether filling space,
Then banished for the elegance of nothing,
I may some day in the journal of your eyes
Read vacuum, and kiss the emptiness

With one last credo of believing lips,
Then turn away to fact, to make my peace,
If peace there is. Or turn to necromancers,
Through some fat medium hear your slender voice—
Telling me what? I ask for no apocalypse

Of revelation. Tell me only (if it is so)
The pear tree blossoms in a hum of bees
Were truly white upon the bough—whether
They flowered fifty years or were a day's
Delight. Tell me this much, and I will let you go.

7

SATORI

"What do you think you're doing here?"
"Dining on fear."
"Be of good cheer."

"Where did you find that morsel to eat?"
"Out in the street."
"First wash its feet."

"What will you do when dinner is through?"
"I'll chew and chew."
"You always knew."

WHEN ADAM HAD NO HISTORY

When Adam had no history
And Eve had even less
It was no trick for the only man
To love the lonely lass.

When Adam had no pantaloons
And Eva no bra and slip
It was no chore to love her well
And tumble sound asleep.

The birds for psychoanalysts
Flew twittering overhead
And tall giraffes like friendly priests
Approved their nuptial bed.

When Adam had no history
And Eve had even less
They loved without the salt of sin
And did not know the loss.

WHEN JESUS CAME TO GALILEE

When Jesus came to Galilee
The neighbors climbed the nearest tree
To see what marvel this might be.

When Jesus came to Cana's feast
They guzzled like a drunken beast
And loved their friends one day at least.

When Jesus walked upon the sea
And shouted gaily, "Walk with me,"
The casualties were two or three.

When Jesus answered, "I am he,"
They shrieked, "Barabbas—set him free!"
And Jesus climbed the drunken tree.

THE SAVIOR SAW THE BLEED OF CRY

The savior saw the bleed of cry.
There was no answer in the sky.
The olive trees were blanched and dry.

Small rodents mumbled in a grave.
Big curses rumbled from a cave.
The dull night grumbled like a slave.

And inchworms ate the book of law.
Palm Sunday's donkey supped on straw.
The high priest ate his shellfish raw.

PURGATORY

Take off your clothes, all of you. Neither male
Nor female enters here. First, a quick shower to cleanse you
Of venial dirt. Now, into the hot room, sit or recline
On the three ranks of benches. 220 Fahrenheit,
230, rising. Splendid. Here are a dipper and a pail.

Throw water on the stove if you like your heat choking.
You are sweating now. Excellent. You will be clean yet.
Take this bundle of birch twigs and scourge your neighbor's
    back.
It stirs the sluggish blood to circulate.
No loud conversation please, no drinking or smoking.

Very good, go jump in the lake between floes of ice,
Swim till you feel like April, then return. Wipe your feet
Before entering the anteroom. You may remain naked or put on
    new robes
As you prefer. There will be light refreshments to eat.
Light up and drink. You may now practice the hymns of
    paradise.

A LIGHT-WEIGHT UNIVERSE

Brave little God
Who undertook like me
To build a universe,
Nails bend, holes magnify
With weight of wood.

Right angles twist obtuse,
Nothing is true.
What you and I have wrought
Is the hubris of the planning mind,
And here it shakes and shivers, of no cosmic use.

Come, little God, with little me
And help me find
The dimestore TinkerToy that I once bought.
Come, lend a tiny hand;
We'll build a light-weight universe and play.

I HAVE BEEN HERE BEFORE

It seems, as I age, that archetypes are all.
This dormitory room and the twin sterile beds,
The window with the draft I can't localize,
The dresser-desk with a Gideon Bible
But no ashtray, the toilet that rumbles a little—
I have been here before, I have seen all this,
If not precisely on other blurring campuses,
Then at least and first in Plato's heaven
Where all archetypes are mounted in plain view
Of the tarrying souls.

Now is the knock on the door, the student
To lead me to breakfast, where I choose waffles
Already limp with the burden of syrup, a sausage
Withered by the heat of age, the vital coffee.
Other students, members of a committee, I think,
Join us with sadly functional trays. At 7:30
We try to talk. I am paid to talk and be talked to.

Chapel is eleven, voluntary these days but strongly
Encouraged by the sideburned with-it chaplain
And his panel of student multimedia liturgists.
Will it be modern dance this time or slides with taped noises?
Or helium balloons rising in metaphors of resurrection?
I can wait to know. My sermon notes are ready;
I have cased the lectern—high enough and steady.
The P.A. is served by an invisible responsibility.

The odd thing—I really believe this stuff,
Or believe I believe it, which is as near sincerity
As one can approach in such matters.
It is odd not to be a hypocrite and sometimes unnerving,
Particularly when people I would least readily seek
For friends smile affirmingly at my words.

79

It is all explained of course, as everything is
By *cur Deus homo.* A videotape of the Savior
Would reveal perhaps an offensive, nasal twang,
A wart to the left of the lower lip, maybe
A compulsive twitch. That incarnation was godly-thorough,
Warts and all. Immanuel is not Hebrew for Adonis.

It is fitting, therefore, that I eat a wither of sausage
And make small talk with a montage of Jesus freaks
And New-Berrigan Christians, and that my snobbery
Ironically observes my snobbery.

THREE HYMNS WAITING FOR MUSIC

1

Praise Him loud and praise Him lowly.
Sidewalks echo to His feet.
Praise Him fast and praise Him slowly,
Alley, avenue, and street.
Praise the honking horns and whistles
Blaring forth the unknown God.
Praise the violets and thistles
Watered green by heaven's blood.

Praise Him in the subdivisions.
Praise Him in the city slum.
Praise Him in the murdered redwoods
And the beating rains that drum
On the rooftops of our terrors
And the windows of our hopes.
Praise Him in our truths and errors
And the ceaseless watch He keeps.

Praise Him in the wolf and rabbit,
In the cockroach and the rat.
Praise Him in the force of habit,
And the fires that level flat
All the suburbs of the manger
Till the kneeling kings are seen
Circled round the sleeping stranger,
And the city streets blaze green.

2

When Mary saw her baby
She took him in her arms.
The ghosts beyond the manger
Waved avenues of palms.
When Mary saw her baby
She took him to her breast.
While carpenters nailed crosses
She nursed his cries to rest.

When Mary saw her baby
He looked like any child,
But kings came in and knelt there,
The shepherds' song was wild,
The donkey twitched his tether
And tried to kneel all fours.
What were the big wings beating
Outside the open doors?

When Mary saw her baby,
She heard the hammers ring,
And palms grew straight and taller;
A bright star paused to sing.
When Mary saw her baby,
She laid the world to rest.
She wrapped him in his swaddling
And laid him at her breast.

3
London Bridge is falling down, down,
Empire State is lying flat.
All the works of hands and hammers
Lie in judgment at His feet.
Mortared stone in which we trusted,
Shafts of reinforced concrete
Prostrate on the earth before Him
And the sky one crimson shout.

Shout of terror, shout of yearning
Rising from each city street.
Runways cracked and smoke from burning
Jets dissolving in their heat.
He is with us. Christ defend us
From the Christ of this return.
Savior, save us from Your double,
From this Christ of burn, burn, burn.

See the sky's polluted evening
Washed to blue by crimson dyes.
See His hand that grasps the trowel,
See the rivets of His eyes.
In the debris of His judgment
Hear the fading groans and moans.
Rise into the air to meet Him.
Be His temple's newfound stones.

THE BLUE MOSQUE

Look up and you look down, sea depth or sky,
Either or both, aloof from common earth.
The tiles in mazes of pure blue and white
Spell Allah who is one and has no son,
And dazzle to submission the world's eye.

Be little here and know that He is great
And clear beyond the blotch of death and sin.
In golden tendrils of His Arabic
Read the bright bands of grace upon the walls,
His Meccan will once spoken. Be and wait.

Your small watch ticks in His eternity.
At His fixed moment the muezzin calls.
Fall like a wheat stem reaped for paradise
And turn the body's eye from blue and white
Who was and is and evermore shall be.

THE INSISTENT GUEST

"Straighten my heart and true it."
"Your heart was always true, I made it so."
"Why does it sag and grumble when creation's hand
Rattles and turns the knob?"
"I'll square the frame, but first, may I come through it?"

"Could you not wait till things are tidied up a bit?"
"Sit down, I'll do the job.
The books in place, your suits hung up in closets.
I'll help you with the boxes. I've lifted heavier weights."
"They're heavy, I admit."

"And now this rug, I'll hang it up and beat it.
One other thing, where do you keep the dinner plates?"
"There in the washer, dirty."
"I made the wet sea and the dirty land.
Here is a plate, a knife and fork, a heart. Eat it."

A CANTICLE OF PRAISE, FEAR, HATE, AND LOVE

To You, who shaped a round ball with your kneading hands
And set the continents upon their floating plates;
To You who built Your thermonuclear reactor
The proper distance for the paradise of lovers
And aimed Your ultraviolet rays, like penises,
To fertilize the vapor, methane, and ammonia,
Begetting amino acids;
To You, I say, be glory, laud, and honor for ever.

To You, who shaped the carbon atom to Your will,
The extrovert of elements, binding itself
To any neighbor in complex societies;
To You, who saw the single cell afloat at sea,
And sang down years of light, "Divide and multiply"
(Behold creation's cell, still living in the lips
That speak these words of praise),
To You, I say, be glory laud and honor for ever.

To You, who knitted cell to cell in moving cities
And from the breathing ocean greened the flinty land;
To You, the Lord of photosynthesis, inventor
Of the spine, the engineer of hands and feet, the winged
Designer of the pterodactyl and the bird,
Creator of the furry little mammal, scampering
Between the feet of dinosaurs,
To You, I say, be glory, laud, and honor for ever.

To you, who smiled the chattering primates into being
And coaxed them down from trees, and taught them
   pair by pair
To win a breakfast of bananas with a stick,
And shape a flint blade sharper than a horned owl's beak;
To You, great Zeus and his Prometheus in one,
Who blazed the walls of dripping caves with flash of fire
And multiplied synapses,
To You, I say, be glory, laud, and honor for ever.

To You, who tantalized the wistful, comic creatures
Into the consonants and vowels of retort,
And listened to blind Homer blaze the fall of Troy;
To You, who fashioned life to feast on bleeding life,
Steerer of horned owl to the chipmunk in his forage,
The carpenter of health, the smith of cancer cell,
Beginning and the end,
To You, I say, be glory, laud, and honor for ever.

To You, who planted in my brain the thalamus
Of reptiles basking in the shallow seas of sun,
And in my skin's contentment on the radiant dock
Make me contemporary with the dinosaurs,
Or in love's bed, sing in my central nervous system
The melody the primal paramecium heard,
The God of love and breed,
To You, I say, be glory, laud, and honor for ever.

To You, turned enemy that day I ate your fruit,
Who with the napalm of your anger set in motion
The flailing sword that barred return to paradise,
Who multiplied the thistles of the desert sands;
To You, who set the caveman at his brush and palette,
And told me, "Shape your paradise of dancing words
Here if at all, east of Eden,"
To You, I say, be glory, laud, and fear for ever.

To You, who shared my exile on a crooked tree
And called Yourself and heard no answer from the sky;
Who gave a dying woman into my mortal arms
And said, "Love one another while two hearts are beating,"
And programed silence timed by craft of genes and chance,
And in the desert of three days of silence left
The universe careening by its laws and habits,
To You, I say, be glory, laud,'and fear for ever.

To You, poor God, in Your infinitudes of art,
Shaping amoeba, crocodile, and me, testing
The relative efficiency of legs and wings,
The slant of teeth, the grip of claws and fangs and hands,
As profligate of raw materials as Your Michel
And his abandoned blocks of chiseled marble failures;
To You, who made nine planets, paused, and peopled one;
To You, I say, be pity, laud, and honor for ever.

To You, deaf God, whose lips stood mute at Calvary,
Who hid Yourself in darkness when I cried to You,
Eli Eli lama sabachthani, to You,
The vulture soaring circles above the battlefield,
The carrion of death, the fetid nursing home—
Lama sabachthani, lama sabachthani,
And still no answer from the vulture's grinning lips,
To You I say—I do not say. To You, to You.

To You the torturer, giver of consciousness,
By which I hear the fish worms in the sodden ground
Singing my welcome to the grave, and every tree
Flexing its roots to aim them at my silent heart;
To You who gave me speech to bless or curse or praise,
And spread before my eyes blue sky, white cloud, green trees
And the ignorant joy of singing birds,
To You I say these words of hate and fear for ever.

To You, experimental God, who visited the death
That You created, lying cold and stiff and blind
Deep in a cave whose walls no dancing animals
Enlivened; You who laid aside the brush and palette,
The T-square and the level, and felt the universe
Plunging into the random void where it began,
To You, who woke barely in time,
To you I say—what do I say?—to you for ever.

To You who stood, a gold gleam in the shine of sun
And rose like rockets aimed at the last edge of space,
Lifting my thoughts and heart beyond the continents
And their slow grind of epochal collisions;
To You, who nowhere, somewhere, everywhere and here,
God of the owl, the chipmunk, God of the touching lovers,
The voice clearer than love's touch,
To You, I say these fumbled words, scattered for ever.

Because I did not make myself, because You planted
Inside my public modesty of shielding skin
A heart that beats without a memo of reminder,
And lungs that barter carbon dioxide for oxygen
While I sleep on, and kidneys regulating acid bases—
The faucet of my inner waterways—because
I lived and moved before I thought,
To You, I say, be glory, laud and honor for ever.

Because You worked by trial and error, testing the meters
And rhymes of every poem You composed, selecting
The laws to be embodied in the book of physics;
Because Your universe is littered with Your failures—
Those crumpled manuscripts akin to my rejections—
Because I am Your poem, and in my freedom speak
Answering verses of praise for love,
To You, I say, be glory, laud, and honor for ever.

Because Your wounded body lay beside mine in a cave,
And hand in hand we walked into the springtime sun,
And hand in hand we blessed the rising grass of life
And called it good; because we rose to where true vision is
And saw the sonnet world, turning in its iambics;
Because my heart was beating with the meter of Your art,
Because Your art is the art of love,
To you be glory, honor, laud, and love for ever.

THE GRAVITY OF THE MATTER

The gravity of the matter,
O grave earth,
The small bones
Weighting my feet
Into molten hell
As though great Jupiter
Summoned me.

The winged thing
Through thin air
Cuts, veers, sinks, rises,
The slight quiver, the wings
On gusts, rivers of sky,
Raising it into high freedom.

How many times
Of earth's mass
Hold me, cold me,
Feet sinking,
Humus, dead things,
Blazing center, molten iron,
Rotating stiff, dark,
Forever in the blank cycle
Of dead day, fast night.

I shall not fly
Save on the shoulders of Christ the gull.
The wing of dust,
The unbegotten wing.

FOR SAVE OF GIVE FORGIVE MY SOUL

For save of give forgive my soul,
For hollow O and empty I,
And hand me down my begging bowl.

For I is hollow as a hole,
And O is sallow as a sky,
O give of save, forgive my soul.

And I of be and do of dole
Are luniac and maria-dry.
Pray hand me down my begging bowl.

Name me your actor. Set the role,
A come of which, a go of why.
O sieve of gave, give me a soul.

A clown of so, a crown of droll,
Rich me with alms and lift them high
From overgo of begging bowl.

O shrive of grave and criss of pole
And dye of death and death of die,
With salve of grieve live me a soul
And hang me up my begging bowl.

A Technical Postscript

In 1967 I was revising the poems that two years later were published as *The End of Nature*. I had been on a formalistic rampage for some time; in particular, I was intrigued by two complicated forms I had invented, the circular sonnet and the quintina.

I began to feel an inner revulsion. Was form becoming an end in itself? This reaction did not surprise me. Several times in my career I had shifted abruptly from strict forms to free, or *vice versa*. But this time there was an added factor. I had recently begun going on poetry tours. Reading my work aloud made me much more aware of the oral-aural character of poetry. Suddenly the obvious occurred to me—Why not create a kind of poetry, free and "organic" in form, and oral/aural from the beginning?

I set up my portable tape recorder and began dictating poems as they welled up from somewhere. Often they came one right after the other. I paid little conscious attention to such niceties as discernible meter, stanza form, or rhyme. The poems simply tumbled out. Later I transcribed them and then put them through the usual revision process with ballpoint and paper, though I sometimes re-recorded them at stages along the way to test their spoken quality. The flood continued off and on for more than two years, and I still occasionally return to the experiment. Meanwhile, what did I learn?

First, that spontaneity is long-winded. I estimate that two-thirds of the tape poems were still windy and flabby even after several revisions. Certainly, one rarely comes out with symmetrical verse forms and concise diction when clutching a microphone. Mostly the poems were very free verse—though now and then a kind of compulsive rhyming, like Mother Goose, would intrude, and at other times the result would be shaped by patterns of line length, repetition of phrases, parallelism of language, etc.

The most interesting discovery was that the tape recorder is an inexpensive psychoanalyst. The dictated poems gradually moved backward in time until I was celebrating events (as early as the age of two or three) that I had not remembered in many decades. Most of these poems were in a subdued, "minor" key. They were usually straightforward, with little play of poetic wit or multiple levels of ambiguity. But some of them were effective poems.

To sum it up: the experiment netted me a handful of poems that I like, and which would probably never have come into existence if I had not taken microphone in hand. The tapepoems that survived my successive revisions and screenings are scattered throughout this book. They are particularly dominant in section 3, where all the poems except the last two were originally taped.

If the involuted circular sonnet and quintina were thesis, and the tapepoem was antithesis, I suppose Hegelian dialectic required the emergence of synthesis, some highly flexible form but still recognizably a form. This occurred in the summer of 1969. I was playing with the idea of doing a long poem, and wanted a stanza form that would create a tension between the autonomy of the individual stanza and the continuous flow of the poem. Terza rima was already available, but I knew from experience how hard that form is to sustain in English without clanking. I decided to dilute it. I increased the number of lines to five, keeping the rhymes farther apart. In each stanza the first and last lines normally rhyme (emphasizing the integrity of the stanza) and the fourth line of a stanza rhymes with the second line of the next (emphasizing the unbroken flow from stanza to stanza). Any other rhyming is *ad lib* and *ad hoc.*

Though I invented the stanza—call it quinta rima—with long poems in mind, I soon found myself using it mostly in short ones, especially those three stanzas in length (quinta rima triplicata?!). And frequently, as will be seen in "Reflections in the Course of an Average Day," "Lunar Love," and "Terrestrial Love," the fifteen-line poems had a way of coming in groups, rather like sonnet sequences.

I tried the new form for a variety of subjects and moods, and indeed it proved versatile, much as the sonnet is. In ways I find hard to put into words, it feels different from the sonnet.

94

It is a shaggier form (particularly when line length and meter are freely varied); it leaves more of a sense of partial resolution, of mysteries yet to explore. Anyway, it became my favorite obsession for several years—and at this very moment I feel an urge to experiment with it further.

One aspect of this intrigues me. When I began experimenting with quinta rima triplicata, John Berryman had already started publishing his dream songs, written in units of three six-line rhymed stanzas. Robert Lowell had fixed on a rhymeless fourteen-line form which he used for individual poems and sequences in *Notebook 1967–68*. I can't recall being influenced by either example. The really astonishing coincidence was when—in the midst of my experiments—I received from my good Roman friend, Edoardo Cacciatore, a copy of his recent book in which he employed a fifteen-line form (divided into three stanzas) that rhymed almost though not quite precisely the same as mine. I began to wonder if there is some collective poetic consciousness at a given period, and if Berryman, Lowell, Cacciatore, and I were all striving to bring into being some new form that would offer a fruitful blend of freedom and form.

Chad Walsh

Notes on the Poems

This book, in an earlier version, was a finalist manuscript in the annual competition of the Virginia Commonwealth/Associated Writing Programs (1976).

Once again I wish to thank the trustees of Yaddo—this time for a month's residence in the spring of 1970. Many of the poems were completed or begun there.

Lunar Love. Space travel is public poetry. My sequence sometimes alludes to specific flights, but does not attempt to maintain the actual chronological order.

On Reading Thompson's Biography of Robert Frost. Some things I wanted to say could be said only in Frost's own words; hence the verbal echoes.

In Memory of W.H. Auden. Obviously written before Robert Lowell's sudden death. Lowell may not have been quite as tall as the other poets I listed; but who now is more than medium height?

Three Hymns Waiting for Music. I am happy to say that these hymns have now been set to beautiful and haunting music by Alec Wyton. "Praise Him Loud and Praise Him Lowly" is available from Randall M. Eagen & Associates, Publishers, Inc., 2024 Kenwood Parkway, Minneapolis, Minnesota 55404, and "When Mary Saw Her Baby" from Augsburg Publishing House, 426 South Fifth Street, Minneapolis, Minnesota 55415.

Acknowledgments

Grateful acknowledgment is made to the periodicals in which many of these poems were first published. In some instances, the poems now appear in revised form or with different titles.

Anglican Theological Review: The Angle of My Eyes
Arizona Quarterly: I Put the Split Beech
Ashland Poetry Press: Pots and Kettles
Beloit Poetry Journal: Lunar Love (part 3)
Carolina Quarterly: In Memory of W.H. Auden; I Have Been Here Before
Chelsea: I Hated My Father
Chicago Tribune: In the Meadow of the Garden of the Squirrel; Lunar Love (part 4)
Christian Century: A Light-Weight Universe; When Jesus Came to Galilee; A Canticle of Praise, Fear, Hate, and Love
Christianity Today: Three Hymns Waiting for Music (1 and 3)
English Record: Lie on the Wooden Planks of the Floor; The Year Before I Started First Grade; When Autumn Came
Hampden-Sydney Poetry Review; On Building a Cradle for Chad Walsh Hamblin
Ktaadn: Reflections in the Course of an Average Day (part 4)
Living Church: Three Hymns Waiting for Music (2)
Lynx: When Old Joe Laid His Banjo Down; For Save of Give Forgive My Soul
Midwest Quarterly: Reflections in the Course of an Average Day (part 1)
Mississippi Review: Courtesy; Zihuatanejo
Nation: The Grant Wood Gothic Turks
New Laurel Review: Terrestrial Love (part 2)
New Orleans Review: Terrestrial Love (part 3)
New Republic: Ascension
New York Times: Sapphics; Peppe; Reflections in the Course of an Average Day (part 3)
Outposts: The Air Rifle I Wanted
Prairie Schooner: Purgatory
Religious Humanism: The Warnings Are so Mild I Could Almost Unsay Them

Review of Books and Religion: When Adam Had No History
Spirit: Widened to the Congo; Vacuous Bliss
Stones: Ecological Aftermath
World Order: Kent; Lament for a Fallen Waxwing